T0166787

LOVE ALGORITHM

Eleni Cay

Love
Algorithm

First published in 2021
by the Black Spring Press Group
Grantully Road, Maida Vale, London W9,
United Kingdom

This imprint: Eyewear Poetry

Typeset with graphic design by Edwin Smet
Author photograph Trond Furenes

ISBN 978-1-913606-01-5

BLACKSPRINGPRESSGROUP.COM

You cannot schedule happiness,
but if you live fully and love purely, you will
gradually unravel the code of a meaningful existence.

Eleni Cay, 2021

TABLE OF CONTENTS

'YOU WANT TO COME TO MINE?'

The sky was bursting with berries, ready to be sipped.
You offered me a cup of tea. I lifted the lid of the pot,
soaked the whole room with succulent peach.

You asked Alexa for Chopin. Mouth open,
I was learning you – my new language – the rhythm
of your eyelashes, the shape of your fingernails,
cracked in the middle like coffee beans.

You kissed me on my right cheek, I pulled
the skein of twisted endings towards the door.
With a command, we have become black quavers,
dots and semi-circles fingered on a Spanish guitar,
the notes in the morning song you hum.

ORANGES ARE THE ONLY FRUIT

My grandfather unwrapped his first orange when he was nine.
He didn't wash his hands till Three Kings' Day,
the sweet essence lingering on his calluses.
He used to say grandma's hugs were like oranges in winter.

My parents plundered a few when they were young.
The bold sweetness of Valencias ignited a land of opportunity
inside their mouths. They gobbled the flesh together
with the skin, blinded by its flushed sun.

Mr McPhee bought as many as the words he wrote for *The New Yorker*,
and cut them into nine like planets or into quarters like lunch
for the businessmen. They tasted to him of a pre-dawn running,
pesticide-rich, fruitless manufactured concentrate.

I have experienced many. Too many oranges for one person to carry.
I calorie-checked, Instagrammed, changed them beyond recognition.
With yellow nails you carved out the seeds. *Now the oranges are mine,*
you said, *no one can put fruit back together once it is cut in half.*

CHANGE OF HEART

We used to meet in a double bed.
Bare feet. Absolute trust. Shared sweat.

These days we meet in busy cafés
with sticky tables and tall skinny lattes.

Anything else I can get you?
The waitress cuts the silence between us.

What was one has turned into two.
What was simple became endless choice.

We used to be lovers,
then we became best friends.

Now we are strangers.
Love story in reverse.

IKTSUARPOK

The July sun cuts the clouds into slices
of a lemony cake, the birds fly through
layer by layer, sculpting our story.

Inuits have a word for looking outside
in anticipation that someone might be coming.
I don't have a special word, I'm just waiting.

Every day, I roll out a royal carpet
where you can ride your Dutch bike,
splash flowers from the wicker basket.

I see the same bike at stations in
Manchester, in Shanghai, run to it,
cycle it back to where we met.

LATE SUMMER EVENING

When it started raining, I knew exactly
where the puddles would be.

> We have tangoed, many times, this street.

A bright red strawberry cuts through the thick
layers of a lemon posset pudding.

> The desire for the silk of your body still tangles my mind.

All these deep holes…

> Who will fill them up?

JOURNEYINGS

It was the end of summer.
You rolled down the car window
poked your head out like a Labrador.

If love does not criss-cross familiar paths,
then I don't know how to remember life.

I press my lips on your jumper, the fabric soft
as your cheeks, the sleeves as long
as your arms waiting for me at the bus stop.

August breaks hearts so that they grow
more resilient. A pen rolls your lips into a poem.

If love does not criss-cross familiar paths,
then I don't know how to remember life.

EVERGREEN CAROL

When I miss you, I get up onto a sleigh,
command reindeers to charge backwards
twenty-three years, reconstruct how you sang
'La Paloma' when braising your pheasant
– without commenting on my vegan soup –
the way you puffed like a bottlenose dolphin
blowing bubble rings when you saw the baby
pig in the woods… the *uh-hum* you grunted
through zipped lips when I talked about
Instagram... I sailed through the Land
of Silence, laughed at your BBC vowels,
swore at your hunt-and-peck on the keyboard…
I still get up at 2am, fluff the empty pillow next to me…
Were your vocal chords bent into a spherical shape or how
come there was such a depth to your voice – and yet
such a high pitch in your off-tune whistling?
I ride in the white land with the jingling
of sounds that even after the freezing halt
can still signal your presence.

ORDINARY ROUTINES

I love brushing my teeth with you.

How we become united in the evening routine,
dedicate all care to the mouths that will soon
sew up the day with a goodnight kiss.

That time of the day where we both belong
and yet maintain our freedoms, each armed
with a differently coloured plastic weapon.

I love how we both start at the same time
up and down, back and forth, checking from
the corner of the eye whether the end is near.

Then one of us makes a strangled noise, a sign
it's time to empty everything into the sink,
rinse it with fresh water and smile with that

beguiling, purifying peppermint.

EARLY SNOW

He rings the doorbell,
climbs the fifteen steps to my flat,
tosses a gluten-free oatcake to my Bichon.

He smiles. Our fingers brush
as he hands me a baronial envelope.
It could be a bill or a tacky sympathy card.

I loathe the people he connects me with.
But I love how he swings between them and me.
It starts snowing. He will be running late. I invite him in.

I offer him a coffee. He tells me he has two daughters. I wonder
how many snowflakes get wasted every year, especially before Christmas.
He is missing a tooth. And all the magic. I want him to leave.

The snowflakes scatter the soundless territory,
they cannot linger in the in-between.
But then, who can?

I watch how the air separates their laced bodies
from the brown soil, how some land
on my postman.

CALEDONIAN SLEEPER

The sun has infused the sky with orange zest.
A girl wraps her arms around the train seat.

Tickets please! She hides beneath a newspaper spread,
today's horrific stories quietly cover her body.

The man in carriage A has finished his sushi. Left-over
sesame seeds shine on her ebony forefinger like stars.

She cuddles her canned soup. The soup responds
with a warm embrace. Chicken, carrot and ginger,

the smell of Christmas. The soup doesn't care about
yesterday's drama or today's saltiness.

The birds sing 'Sweet Home Alabama'.
She ducks in every time the train manager passes by.

DINING WITH A HOMELESS MAN FROM HOVE

He orders two starters.
No alcohol, just food.

He would request the whole menu
if he could. He tries to eat quietly

but each bolus tumbles
like a heavy coin in a deep well.

I got the liver pâté for you!
He treats me with what I treated him.

I struggle to hold the fork in my right hand,
try to swear now and then. Get at his level.

He talks about a new spot at the station
— *It's warm there and free toilets.*

If he had one of those Ralph Lauren shirts
(and better teeth), would I fall for him?

I must be boring to you, he glances
at my fake wedding ring.

What am I compensating for?
For being born, for growing up in privilege?

The fat from the pork rind runs down
his lower lip. I think of our carnal equality.

We are NOT equal.
I have my safety net, cushions.

All he has is cardboard and a Bible.
I am glowing, he is invisible.

But his hands… they tremble as much as mine.
Who will measure, ascertain

the fear that this could happen to anyone?
We are all caught up in the same rat-race;

the plutocrats got us all. Is this what unites us?
Eat up. It's just one dinner. That's what you agreed upon.

LONGING FOR NEVERLAND

I used to compete for your attention
with Jackie, Rebecca, Jill and Kate.

I knew their secrets, bra sizes, what time
they would meet you at the school gate.

Today, a billion girls live in your pocket,
beating me thin, to almost transparent.

I want to go back, back to the times
when we would kiss under the bridge,

both of us believing in the whirl
we darted on like Tinker Bell to a water lily.

A SINGLE BROAD BRUSHSTROKE

I remember my classmate Adrian.
He couldn't make sums of the present.
Twenty, twenty-one, twenty-two,
he'd been counting the days to Christmas.
To New Year's Eve. To his birthday.
Then complained that the gifts never came.

He used to wear a beret, sombrero, sun hat,
all three stacked on top of each other.
When his slight hands overlapped with Miss Willams',
she let him fill the voids between clouds.
He stuffed them with gold statues of gods,
argued they evidenced peace and wars.

South, east, north, west, he always held a compass
in his hand, rubbing and buffing its lid,
following the needle even when upside down.
He placed the distant points directly opposite
the starting points, took his enemies, avatars, head-on,
replicated hierarchies in worlds meant to be virtual.

Then, one day, Adrian swallowed his compass –
the navigation arrows blemished his skin,
blue and red lines indicated the bearing to follow.
He became quiet. Miss Willams said his mind grew
into a Zen-like oasis. It had all come together for him.

AT THE STUDENT UNION CAFÉ BAR

The professor mapped cloud journeys
to four cardinal directions.
Colours of leaves to four seasons.

Said that snowflakes are just molecules
attracting each other through
Newton's predictable laws.

You wink back at me. We take
the legs of the coffee table,
return them to trees.

The waiter pixelates us for his website.
Our kiss rises up with the steam
of our coffee to the bitter

blueness of the sky. The moon makes
the motorway a river in which we can
swim how we like before we drown.

DIGITAL DIVIDE

Knock, knock, your dinner is ready! I peer into the darkness behind your door.
I hear you laugh, I hear you curse, but you can't hear me with your headset on.

Your friend Nicky368, your rok followers and avatars, will they know you when
your battery is flat? Can we invite them over, meet their parents, have a chat?

I try my hardest to join the fun; I send you my first tweet. You say it's hilarious
and want to Facebook it. I know that things have changed: I trim my fingernails

to remove the soil from gardening, you trim them so that you can better glide
on the screen. God personified into the Internet: omniscient and omnipresent

codes guide your moves. But one thing hasn't changed: I want to do the best
for you. And I worry about the deep scars in your mind. What can I do – make

new rules for you to break? Play catch with each new game? I give up. I shout:
Your dinner is ready young man! You smirk at me: *Could've sent me an email?*

I blog: *This is a chasm, not a generation gap!* You text: <3 *Love you dad.*

MILLENNIAL

The human mind operates in binary.
So it should be easy to survive the votes,
to choose between red or blue borders, leaders.
Purple hybrids don't have to choose
between zeroes and ones. Flashing
their bodies on IG they pretend
to be a new animal – before the darkness comes.

DIVORCE

When you and dad argued in the garden, I chewed the teddy's right ear off,
so that he wouldn't hear you cry. You didn't want to talk about mending,

you said there are many teddies like him. He held my hand when I was alone,
when I waved at you from Mrs Gill's window. He knew exactly how many

forbidden sweets and how many monsters were hidden under my pillow.
I lost him on a muddy pavement one rushed morning. I cried, wanted to

know why and where he was. You taught me to be a grown-up. You said,
There is no reason, it's just because. We have to carry on, let others pick him up.

DIGITAL LOVES

Oblivious to the morning chit-chat
of roses climbing the north-facing wall,
a white iPhone blasts a techno tune.

Miss Wrong wakes up, swipes right.
Mr Wrong sends her a kiss emoticon.
His protein biceps balloon,

as she announces they are 'in a relationship.'
120k likes from their Facebook friends
seal their status Mr and Miss Right *Now*.

Declarations ebb and flow in algorithms.
New holiday selfies hang in the gallery of air.
But love narratives do not follow scheduled

serendipity. When they break up
there are no suitcases by the door:
just a switch flicked on an invisible wall.

The roses quiet their scented talk,
put the day to sleep, their skin glowing
from an overheated screen.

WIRELESS FOR FREE

On their first date, she was impressed
that he didn't ask for her Facebook avatar,
that he was more interested in her presence
than her past faux-pas. To offer her exactly
what she liked, he waited to hear it from her mouth.

After their first date, he was impressed
that it's a real female voice that greets him
every morning. That she too, knows his diary,
can visualise his thoughts, check the weather,
order anything or nothing.

Once they'd tried it
they couldn't live without it.
They've searched for it everywhere,
would pay a premium to have it –
unlimited – or be cut off completely.

OUR DICTIONARY

The lovers are *swooping* – it's *their* word
for love-making. They are interlacing
oxygen molecules in a kiss, making their own air.

Radio 4 plays U2's 'Beautiful Day'. It's *their* song.
They cemented it into the Versailles Metal
of the French café you pass by every morning.

She makes his favourite chocolate cake, takes a few
familiar ingredients, beats them until smooth,
then spreads them evenly between two layers.

I love the filling. She cushions the sound
coming from between his lips with her tongue.
How you make it. How we eat it. Everything.

THE MOON AND THE SUN ON TINDER

In the mass market of galaxies,
the Moon was unsure whom to like.
Her resources were limited.
She could not afford a golden account.

The Sun knows the game,
he has swiped right.
Perhaps the mysterious algorithm
is not that smart.

CRASH

I remember the shimmer of every tree we passed on the motorway.
The exact number of the small wrinkles around your lips.

Each of us in our own seats, together in our shared mobile house.
We had sandwiches, music – and we had us.

Nothing else mattered, until the drop of water on the windscreen
changed from a raindrop into a red splash.

PROFILE UPDATE

Our intertwined selves did not transcend
the little while between two hearts' beats

      – they became double and separated.

And we, it seems, yet another couple
with the Facebook status *It's complicated*.

MIRROR OPPOSITES

I touch-typed love poems on your chest,
lipread passion from your eyes, covered
my inexperience behind the white duvet,
striped it with my mascara. You stayed for
breakfast, had a spoonful of diet yoghurt,
teased me that I had no eggs or milk. You
sat on the kitchen windowsill, the sun was
behind your back, illuminating your hair,
like feathers ready to fly.

Over months, the memory you'd planted
in my brain grew bigger, eating me from
within. I took it out, walked it online,
distracted myself with others in the virtual
playground. But the boulevard twisted
the memory into a wild animal, ravaging
the online streets, killing the meanings of *love*,
friends, invading all the intangible
beauties that make children look like angels.

NIGHT ZOO

It was the time of the month when the Moon
reveals just nine inches of her calcite bust.
We found ourselves in our prisons again:
me in my suffering hutch – you in your guilt
cage. We both betrayed the promise not to
vacate words from thoughts.

Now, neither of us is ready to click and open
a new page, to enjoy our smooth bodies
chest on chest. Instead, we give our offerings
to the thin altars in our hands, we let them break
our hyperlinked memories, hasten the hidden
hotspots in our minds.

We do not own any of the fragments we retrieve,
we don't know the length of their path. We access
what we think is love but can't orient ourselves,
so just give back exactly what we find. The browser
crashes all the time and leaves us with our wings
clipped, unable to fly.

LOVE ALGORITHM

Zara walks her accessorised Dalmatian.
The skyscrapers draw rectangular shadows.

1-0-1-0, dot or line, dot or line, 1-0-1.

The cleaner sweeps cigarette ends,
together with pure white petals.

1-0-1-0, dot or line, dot or line, 1-0-1.

Autumn leaves fly together with plastic bags,
share with them the tiny space on trimmed magnolias.

1-0-1-0, dot or line, dot or line, 1-0-1.

A birch tree moves from left to right
formulating love into black and white.

CITY ABSENCES

Mr Brown buys dinners for two
and gets fat because he is just one.

Neither a woman nor a cat in his bed –
he takes a hot water bottle instead.

He pays extra for more space airborne
and on the ground. And yet, there is no

space for a peacock butterfly in his house.
No time for old books and their curled pages

that resemble hearts. He learnt to care
no longer for the images of dead bodies and billions

of unread words recycled every morning,
with a pair of wings occasionally

– a heartbeat from you and me.

SAN FRANCISCO

The ticket is called Clipper.
The bus is Muni.
The city is SF.

You need to talk in shortcuts
or in brands to be one of us.
Above all, you need to use apps.

Blink for a remote brain scan,
tap for finishing a school exam,
don't move for Uber to pick you up.

We have democracy here, you know.
As long as you have dollars,
everything is equal.

Sebamed, Prozac, a Colt 45
can be bought from the same aisle.
You choose what you spend your dollars on.

Ignore the sunset –
it can't be personalized.
Our tech knows you inside-out.

The more you look, the more precisely
it takes money from your account.
It's so smart that we call it art.

POST-BREXIT THURROCK

A rooftop mirror reflects sunrays
so pedestrians get some vitamin D
between the Council's shadows.

Watch your heart rate, step, breathing,
code yourself into a perfect post,
then disconnect from the world in a

mindfulness class. Exhale through
your hardware, inhale through your soft brain,
relax, everything is under control:

CCTVs tackle crime, Ginkgo trees pollution.
There is no money for prevention, fake it
till you make it, austerity came to town.

Wrestling posters go all the way up
to the cancelled poetry festival,
wearing down a ripped off Union Jack.

People converse less, compete more.
A fat man looks at his fat son.
If he could, he would suck him to bone.

IN THIS CITY

dogs have fenced-off areas
where they can run, adults
where to work, where to make
love. No one is free to roam.

Amputated trees are nurtured
by a designated member of staff.
They are watered at fixed intervals –
like the elderly in nursing homes.

Teddy bears are hauled around in
plastic bags. All gifts need an
occasion, holidays a set of hashtags.
Silent requests are a rare commodity

in this city.

WHO LISTENS TO THE SANTIAGO SONATA?

Pills, sanitary pads, veg –
all cost too *mucha plata*.
Too long working hours,
too short maternity leave.

Too many dogs that
belong to no one, too many
abandoned books, shoes, children,
graffiti tagging broken promises.

Too many houses no one cares
about, piled-up filth rotting.
'Too many immigrants' from
Peru, Colombia, Haiti.

The very rich live in the cordillera
with breathable air, a few tiles
in Lapis lazuli – deep blue – as if
the sky solidified into a tombstone.

POPLARS

I saw you in Moscow. We exchanged numbers we
knew we'd never dial. You told me how you live on coffee
and twisted relations with time. I can't remember what
I told you about me. Or whether I even drank my tea.

Since then, I can see your face behind windows,
on every screen. The car lights blind me,
I play with them with my half-closed eyes,
make them into luminous rings, our wedding.

I can't make decisions, like a doe in the middle
of the road, unsure whether to cross or not,
never having seen anything that bright.
Then a blaring horn forces me to open my eyes wide.

I see the southeast winds that have been gestating
for fifteen years, applying pressure on
the poplar's branches, every winter daring the roots,
until the tree fell down.

GULLIVER'S NEW TRAVELS

I've become a lover to many women
but none in particular. The more women
I sleep with, the more I miss one.

I'm homeless, yet home-full.
There are no people I know, no people
I miss here nor in my birth town.

The drunken nights in Lille, the lost hour in Berlin
all blur into one big room. I'm a citizen
of everywhere but nowhere in particular.

When I get lonely I find solace in the familiarity
of the global goods around me. I know that dress,
that Alfa Romeo, that Primark shop window.

Or I find comfort online, in the digital home
we all share. My family and friends are there –
well most of the time anyway.

MAYFAIR

We walk against the wind of late November.
Spring has been evicted and the air feels like a gauze,
thin and absorbent, barely covering the Chinese take-away,
a last-minute Dior puff before the Friday night begins.

Shall we try Le Gavroche tonight? You book the table
before my reply. I don't recognise the face on my silver-plated
cutlery. *I feel so cold tonight.* The waiter adjusts the fan,
the air feels sliceable. *Would you like some more?*

FOX BEHIND A STEAMED WINDOW

There is no way in, there is no way out.
I don't want to live between the domesticated and the wild.

Will you tame me?

You are busy cooking and you mistake my tail for a squirrel.

Will you understand me?

I wish I had eyelids and could blink at you and ask:

Will you love me?

THE BLOSSOM

A young cherry tree swans over the Fulham street,
its branches grafted into each other to escape

the brick wall. People say *how pretty*; no one
can see that it has started eating its own body, that

the sullen wind made its petals so small, so small.
Its limbs are broken and veins pulse in strong

bergamot notes. People say *lovely scent;* no one
knows that the tree inside is structured for pain,

that to burn well, it needs to be so hollow, so hollow.

SEX AND THE CITY

When Cupid gets bored
he shoots arrows for one-night stands.
He sends emoticon hearts
from the quadratic beds of budget hotels.

He makes men wear his fragrance,
use his tricks, make their own drugs.
So that love-making feels the same.
Just without the magic dust afterwards.

MONEY, MONEY, MONEY

Our daughter had more hugs from her
Canadian babysitter than from you.
She shares with her books, apps.
All we share are the keys to our big house.

The Swarovski necklace from you feels like
a dog's collar with a magnet. Our cleaner knows
what you wear, Amazon knows what you like.
All I know is the figure in our shared account.

In the Seychelles, we miss fast-speed Internet.
You relax with the small masseuse,
I pretend I'm asleep. When we return home,
you say you liked it that the hotel was so cheap.

WUMBLETOWN'S MONICA

When the news broke that you'd slept with your
young intern, I was prepared to assume the role
of an ostracised victim. But the Internet interfered.

Your affair now ranks top in the Wumbletown's
search results. Higher than the centuries-old church
or Jackson's Pottery and its ecological porcelain.

When people google our town, they get your face.
Everyone can read about her lipstick on my pillow,
the Durex in the bin. A mega trace we would never get

if we stayed together. Our love life is now a commodity
others can trade. That's how it works on the Internet.
In fame and in shame – always and forever.

PARIS IS WORTH 11 POINTS

The Dictionary inhales past hurts, signs them off
for a silent flight, fixes them to closed lips, windows,
river banks.

As if sensing the rhythm of Mozart's *Paris Symphony*,
a poem wriggles up the city's lungs, ready to have its
personality edited, erased.

But before it enters the lexicon, you hold its identity,
guard it against hastened tongues, Twitter feeds. You,
with your warm flesh

and sleek boxes. Let others Scrabble their own stories, then
exhale the unspoken – the only thing that is yours but you
can never own.

MORNING IN SOHO

Energy drink supply runs low with the morning joggers.
They up their pace, get in tune with the accelerated heartbeat –
with the fastest taxi, quickest cleaning service, coffee to grab and go.

The homeless Romanian doesn't care about time. He's happy
with pizza and cheap wine at 6am, his party time scheduled
by a clink of coins, not incoming mail in a work inbox.

Your footfall barely touches the shared filth of the street.
You pay a lot to avoid it. For slowing down. For silences.
The richer you get, the more money you spend on these.

Good morning! Your escort greets you through gritted teeth.
Her morning breath drowned in mouthwash. You jump for
a quick shower. You hate the smell of a human.

HUMAN COST

You had a stressful day: Jenn spilled a coffee on your computer.
The shock was so profound, you had to re-apply your make-up.

Asha had no stress today: no one assaulted his sister. The dust on his face,
deposited over several days, makes him look older, almost dead.

You click away, get the shoes Anne bought last week. Rate
your followers, be only associated with the high players.

There's Asha's face again. Amnesty International says
he's toiled cobalt since he could crawl. His spinal discs are shattered.

You never carry a thing. You've so much in your account
you only ever need your phone. You google for a cashmere coat.

But there's Asha's face again. A Don Bosco lady says he needs
new shoes and books. In her story he is called Ismail.

You block the ad, report abuse. You're one of the gods,
those who are ranked highly will go higher again, those are the rules.

Where am I in this game? Asha will never read, never understand,
this poem. I'm just cleansing my heart from the silver-grey blood.

DECADENCE

The waters that pool in Stockholm's veins
never reach the thirsty Congo girl.
Love flows with no destination,
like a plastic bottle in an urban creek,
its rented body filled with foreign liquids.
So, Tinder, on which beat will you break my heart today?
Will you pierce the soft sling of hope,
let its salt crack open the raw flesh of flirtation?
The kiss Yves owes me winds its way down
to the lips of Gabrielle, to my Gauloises, to a corrupted hell.

SOLDIERS' GRAVES

Inside the innocent poppy heads
there are billions of small black bullets.

Their unrequited kisses
leave empty spaces between the wild rye.

It doesn't matter how many you hurt in the combat.
The fleeting sunset does it every evening to the sky.

What unites us is the red blood,
setting out from the heart.

AUGMENTED BRAINS

The known is finite, the unknown infinite; intellectually we stand on an islet
in the midst of an illimitable ocean of inexplicability.
– T. H. Huxley, 1887

Sedimented in flesh before,
some bedraggled, some ready to bud,
private notes expanded to the digital sky.
You are not sure where the filaments
cross, where they begin. Yet, you thicken
them, make them run faster, determine
how to curate your digital soul.
The templates are the same:
you want to control, make each
piece of materiality searchable, uniform.
You want to augment love, the infinity
within you, within humankind.
The clouds are too heavy to hold all
that stuff without a storm.

THE DIGITAL SELF

At the end of the journey, you will find
an orchid-scented forest
with invisible fairies, dancing en pointe
in emerald leotards on top
of the pine trees. Rest
your little feet, bury
your soft skin in the fairies' pulpy cheeks,
draw heartlets with tears running from your eyes
down to their raspberry lips.

Beware the black sleek boxes
squaring what you can see.
They seize the ballerinas, force
them to dance on steel ropes, break
their wings into programmable threads, turn
them into poison from black fangs.
You too have been stung, your blue-tinged
hair catches on their knife. The fairies dance
within you, tracing a curling pattern of life.

THE KNOWLEDGE OF EVERYTHING

Swifts sleep, mate, eat and feed in the air.
They cut the sky with their scythe tails, lay
the clouds on blue fields in layers of ivory white.

You need a shelter. Marked roads. Shepherds
and machines to craft them to immaculate.
Still, there are holes in your roofs and paths –

and you can't even see them. The knowledge
that cast you out of Eden is merely a foundation
for the boundaries of your soul. The forces

that steer your addictions cross
with the God you domesticated in
the gaps between your thoughts.

THE BLUE FLOWER OF DESIRE

You said *I will love and leave you* and journeyed on.
I was supposed to *keep calm and carry on*.

To sing 'Lavender's Blue' to our baby girl. To run
for and around her, my feet getting blue, my chest

flat and curved forward. I have left my Dior on pillows
of random men, envied them the sleep I haven't had

since you left. I hated silence. I bridled it with Adele,
Metallica, Presley. I drove around the block for hours,

then entered my rented flat and admitted to myself that
our shared history is dieseled on misremembered memory.

JOB INTERVIEW FOR LOVE

Have a seat on a grain of dust. Make yourself at home.
Don't worry about your appearance. The love angels
will patch up all flaws, decide on your golden hours,
dance them into a sweet circle like bees in a honeycomb.

Stretch your feet, scrape off the mud of rejections,
don't worry about your selling points. The angels are not
interested in whatever dwells on the shores of your memory,
nor the tissue-like possibilities of what could have been.

Smile. Lean your bones against their warm wings.
Don't worry about your lack of experience. They will
not grade your efforts. They will lie down on your chest,
listen to your melody, then offer you a permanent position.

A BURNING DESIRE FOR QUESTION MARKS

When your magnifying glass breaks and burns a hole
in your stark-white sheet of paper,
will you begin to honour the distance that separates
glass and wood?

Will you stop measuring success by the weight of water
on your face, or how many colours you sewed
to yourself when walking by the *Angelica*, bluebells
and Jacob's ladders?

If you choose to live between scented meadows and
high mountains, then the City of Curiosity will welcome
you with a warm light, glinting on the trillions of paths
within your wondering mind.

THE LAST POST

I am exchanging the outer and inner,
the virtual and physical selves,
re-posting my genes into another body.
She's now re-tweeting my words
into your inbox. The algorithms
spread the content across the world,
there's no end to an infinite amount.
Her emoticons travel from her to me,
from me to you, from you to your ex,
it's a perpetuum mobile chain of love.

So when I'm gone, erase it all from my account.
The holes inside my quiet bones will remain intact.

NOTES

'Blossom', page 45:

At this season, the blossom is out in full now… and instead of saying 'Oh that's nice blossom'… last week looking at it through the window when I'm writing, I see it is the whitest, frothiest, blossomest blossom that there ever could be, and I can see it. The nowness of everything is absolutely wondrous, and if people could see that, you know. There's no way of telling you; you have to experience it, but the glory of it, if you like, the comfort of it, the reassurance.

– Dennis Potter, 'Seeing the Blossom' interview with Melvyn Bragg, broadcast by Channel 4, April 5th 1994. Transcript from *The Guardian* online, September 12th 2007, 'Great Interviews of 20th Century: We tend to forget life can only be defined in the present tense.'

ACKNOWLEDGMENTS

'Oranges are the Only Fruit' was published in *Poetry Ireland Review* (Issue 125), July 2018. 'At the Student Union Café Bar' was published in *Atrium*, March 2018. 'Soldiers' Graves' was published in *Glasgow Review of Books* in 2016. 'Digital Divide' won the Carefree Kids National Poetry Competition, judged by Rowan Williams in 2016. 'Evergreen Carol' was shortlisted in the Bedford International Writing Competition 2018 and published in the *Cardiff Review*. 'Early Snow' and 'Caledonian Sleeper' were published in *Dodging The Rain* in 2018. 'Iktsuarpok' was highly commended in Poetry Space Competition, judged by Caroline Price in 2019. 'Our Dictionary' was highly commended in the Hastings LitFest writing competition judged by John McCullough.

CPSIA information can be obtained
at www.ICGtesting.com
Printed in the USA
FSHW011143141021
85451FS

9 781913 606015